Like a Bird

To Jim, Anne, and Becky,
who taught me to see
—C.G.

I dedicate this book to every young
mind that dares to be different.
It is my hope that this book will
reflect and engage. I also dedicate
this book to my mother, Karolyn A.
Mitchell, who bought me my first
Harriet Tubman paperback book
when I was a child. Thank you for
planting a seed.
—M.W.

Like a Bird

THE ART of the AMERICAN SLAVE SONG

written by **CYNTHIA GRADY**

concept and art by **MICHELE WOOD**

M MILLBROOK PRESS · MINNEAPOLIS

Much thanks to Dr. Rosita M. Sands, Professor of Music, Columbia College Chicago, and Melanie Zeck, Managing Editor of the *Black Music Research Journal,* Center for Black Music Research, for reviewing this book and offering their insight.

Author's acknowledgments: I am indebted to Michael Henderson and Hilary Hogan of Sidwell Friends School, Kevin Lavine at the Library of Congress, Stephen Henry at the University of Maryland Performing Arts Library, Thad Garrett of Catholic University, and literary agent Caryn Wiseman.

Music engravings by Ted Moore.
Photos in this book courtesy of the Library of Congress.
Bible passages quoted come from the *New International Version.*

Millbrook Press
A division of Lerner Publishing Group, Inc.
241 First Avenue North
Minneapolis, MN 55401 USA

For reading levels and more information, look up this title at www.lernerbooks.com.

Designed by Danielle Carnito.
Main body text set in Chaparral Pro 12/16.
Typeface provided by Adobe Systems.
The illustrations in this book were created with acrylic.

Library of Congress Cataloging-in-Publication Data

Names: Grady, Cynthia. | Wood, Michele.
Title: Like a bird : the art of the American slave song / art by Michele Wood ; text by Cynthia Grady.
Description: Minneapolis : Millbrook Press, 2016. | Includes bibliographical references. | Description based on print version record and CIP data provided by publisher; resource not viewed.
Identifiers: LCCN 2015046001 (print) | LCCN 2015043907 (ebook) | ISBN 9781512408898 (eb pdf) | ISBN 9781467785501 (lb : alk. paper)
Subjects: LCSH: African Americans—Music—History and criticism—Juvenile literature. | Slaves—United States—Songs and music—History and criticism—Juvenile literature.
Classification: LCC ML3556 (print) | LCC ML3556 .G73 2016 (ebook) | DDC 782.25/3—dc23

LC record available at http://lccn.loc.gov/2015046001

Manufactured in the United States of America
1-37901-19174-3/1/2016

*W*hat does a bird have to do with American slave songs? Harriet Tubman, born into slavery around 1820, used to dream that she was flying over the landscape "like a bird." Tubman successfully escaped in 1849 and later helped many others escape to the North. Her dreams echo a phrase that appears in the Bible in Psalm 124:7, "We have escaped like a bird out of the fowler's snare."

The lives of enslaved Africans were extraordinarily difficult, but they were not without song. Africans brought their musical and religious traditions with them to the American colonies. Whether working on ships or docks, in forests or fields, slaves sang. The music helped them pace their movements, lift their spirits, and communicate with one another. Music was important at other times too—they sang together in their cabins and during private times of worship.

Slave owners had never heard such harmonies and syncopated rhythms. Over the centuries, thousands of enslaved people improvised songs to work by and songs to dance to. As slaves slowly adopted the Christian faith of their masters, their songs combined stories from the Bible with African rhythms. These songs of worship are called spirituals.

The Jubilee Singers of Fisk University in Nashville, Tennessee, began performing spirituals in 1871. They toured widely and helped call attention to this musical form.

Musicians, religious leaders, and scholars have worked to preserve the folk songs from this time. The spirituals have received particular attention. Today they are sung in homes, in churches, at schools, and on concert stages around the world.

On the pages that follow, artist Michele Wood has painted her interpretations of thirteen spirituals. The illustrations show people working, dreaming, spying, and rejoicing. You'll find music and lyrics alongside the paintings, as well as brief notes describing biblical, historical, or artistic elements within. Full song lyrics are included at the end of the book.

Sometimes I Feel Like a Motherless Child

On many southern plantations, enslaved people of all ages were forced to pick cotton by hand. This exhausting work began at daybreak and lasted until nightfall—or longer, if the moon was full and bright. Children often worked beside adults with the same long sacks slung over their shoulders. Notice how, in this painting, the children are framed so that the only adult visible is the plantation overseer.

The rhythm and lyrics of "Sometimes I Feel Like a Motherless Child" express longing and despair, making it one of the most haunting songs to come out of slavery. Yet some scholars believe this is a hopeful song. What signs of hope can you find in the lyrics or the painting?

Lamentoso

Some-times I feel like a moth-er-less child,____ Some-times I
Some-times I feel like I'm al - most gone,____ Some-times I
Some-times I feel like a moth-er-less child,____ Some-times I

feel like a moth-er-less child,____ Some-times I feel like a
feel like I'm al - most gone,____ Some-times I feel like I'm
feel like a moth-er-less child,____ Some-times I feel like a

moth-er-less child,____ A long way____ from home.
al - most gone,____
moth-er-less child,____

Ezekiel Saw the Wheel

The people in the Bible's Hebrew scriptures are the source for many of the lyrics and images in spirituals. Ezekiel, a Hebrew prophet, was captured in Judah, his homeland, and forced to work in Babylonia. While he was a captive, Ezekiel had visions of God that included several wheels and winged creatures rising into the sky. As is the case with most folk songs, the lyrics to "Ezekiel Saw the Wheel" have changed over time. Here, the artist has illustrated the "spokes of humankind" described in a later version of the song.

Jacob's Ladder

In the book of Genesis, Jacob leaves his home and dreams of a ladder, or stairway, connecting heaven and earth. God's angels are shown ascending the stairway. Jacob believes his dream is a renewal of God's promises—that the Israelites would form a great nation in a land of their own.

Historians agree that only a small percentage of people ever successfully escaped slavery. For those who spent their entire lives in bondage, climbing Jacob's ladder through song became their way into an eternal life of God's love and protection.

Michael, Row the Boat Ashore

The popular "Michael, Row the Boat Ashore" was originally a work song sung in the Georgia Sea Islands off the coast of South Carolina. Some historians consider it a sacred song as well, with "Michael" referring to the biblical archangel, who would aid the rowers in times of physical or spiritual need.

Take a close look at this painting. Do you see the "panes" of water? This stained-glass waterway is filled with additional biblical symbols.

Mi - chael, row the boat a-shore, Hal-le - lu - jah! Then you'll
Then you'll hear the trum-pet sound, Hal le lu jah! Trum - pet
Trum-pet sound the ju - bi - lee, Hal-le - lu - jah! Trum - pet

hear the trum - pet blow, Hal - le - lu - jah!
sound the world a - round, Hal - le - lu - jah!
sound for you and me, Hal - le - lu - jah!

Nobody Knows the Trouble I've Seen

Slave owners routinely sold and separated family members. In this painting, a mother grieves for her baby, who has been sold to another owner and who will grow up never knowing a mother's love. Even so, this spiritual still imagines an eventual joyous reunion. The dove in the painting is a reminder of God's promise made in John 14:18: "I will not leave you as orphans" without a family or a place to call home.

No-bo-dy knows the trou-ble I've seen, No-bo-dy knows but
No-bo-dy knows the trou-ble I've seen, No-bo-dy knows but
No-bo-dy knows the trou-ble I've seen, No-bo-dy knows but

Je - sus, No-bo-dy knows the trou-ble I've seen, Glo - ry, Hal - le -
Je - sus, No-bo-dy knows the trou-ble I've seen, Glo - ry, Hal - le -
Je - sus, No-bo-dy knows the trou-ble I've seen, Glo - ry, Hal - le -

fine

lu - jah! Some-times I'm up, some-times I'm down, Oh, yes, Lord, Some-
lu - jah! If you get there be - fore I do, Oh, yes, Lord, Tell
lu - jah!

DC al fine

times I'm al - most to the ground, ___ Oh, yes, Lord
all my friends I'm com - ing too, ___ Oh, yes, Lord

Go Down, Moses

Harriet Tubman was known as the Moses of her people. Just as Moses led the Israelites out of slavery in Egypt, Tubman led her fellow slaves to freedom. She believed God spoke to her through dreams and visions, telling her where and when it was safe to travel without being caught by bounty hunters.

During one treacherous journey, Tubman left a frightened group in the woods while she went for food. She returned later filled with the light of God and singing "Go Down, Moses" to assure the runaways that they were safe in her capable hands.

Get On Board— the Gospel Train

The word *gospel* means "glad tidings" or "good news" and refers to the life of Jesus of Nazareth. The "train" in this song is a metaphoric train, not a real one. This song tells us that good news— the message of the New Testament—is rolling through town and anybody is welcome to it. But what do the gestures and facial expressions of the figures in the painting on the previous pages tell you?

Harriet Tubman, at the front of the train, *is* bringing good news. Using her dreams and the North Star to guide her, she is leading her "passengers" to freedom along the Underground Railroad, another metaphoric train.

Harriet Tubman was a conductor on the Underground Railroad, a secret network of people who helped slaves reach freedom in the northern states or Canada. This photograph was taken sometime between 1860 and 1875.

The Gos-pel train's a-com-ing,__ I hear it just at hand, I
I hear the train a-com-ing,__ She's com-ing round the curve, She's
The fare is cheap and all can go, The rich and poor are there, No

hear the car wheel rum-bling,__ And roll-ing through the land.
loos-ened all her steam and brakes, And strain-ing eve-ry nerve.
sec-ond class a-board this train, No diff-erence in the fare.

Chorus

Get on board lit-tle chil-dren, Get on board lit-tle chil-dren, Get on

1.
2.

board lit-tle chil-dren, There's room for man-y more. more.

Deep River

Rivers run throughout the history of slavery, its literature, and its music. The river symbolizes both bondage and independence. When slaves were separated from their families at auction, they were often sent by steamboat down the Mississippi River. Meanwhile, runaways could reach freedom by crossing the Ohio River, a dividing line between several northern and southern states. And throughout the South, Christian congregations gathered along waterways to participate in the rite of baptism, just as people long ago had gathered at the Jordan River where Jesus was baptized.

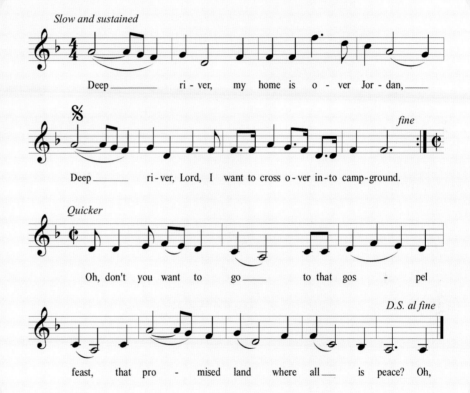

Ain't Gonna Study War No More

Enslaved men fought and spied on both sides of the American Revolutionary War, which lasted from 1775 to 1783. James Lafayette served as a spy for the colonists while masquerading as a spy for the British. Posing as a runaway slave, Lafayette became a servant to British officers in their camps. The officers spoke freely about their battle plans in front of Lafayette. He then gave the information he gathered to other spies working for the colonists. This information was key to the colonists' defeat of the British at Yorktown, which was the final major battle of the war.

Swing Low, Sweet Chariot

Many runaway slaves received shelter, food, and transportation from those who opposed slavery. John Rankin was a minister and abolitionist who built his house on a hill above the Ohio River. His family helped more than two thousand people reach freedom between 1828 and 1864. One hundred wooden steps led up to his home, where he would display a lantern to welcome runaways arriving at night. Abolitionists might have seemed like a "band of angels" to those on their way to the North.

Steal Away

In the 1820s, Nat Turner began having dreams urging him to lead an armed revolt against nearby slave owners. Eventually, Turner decided to fight for his freedom. To arrange secret meetings with other slaves to plan the uprisings, Turner hummed a line from "Steal Away" at sundown. Another slave would pick it up and pass it on, until they all knew a meeting was planned.

Turner's Virginia rebellion in 1831 was one of the most violent in the history of slavery: more than fifty slave owners were killed. Afterward, most of the rebels and many suspected rebels were executed. In response, Virginia and North Carolina created even stricter laws limiting what slaves could do. Turner himself was arrested, tried in court, and sentenced to death, but his song lives on.

Joshua Fit the Battle of Jericho

Joshua was one of the heroes of Hebrew scriptures. This song celebrates his success in leading the Israelites to invade the walled city of Jericho in Canaan, the land promised to them by God. Enslaved people identified with this longing for a land of their own. The walls of slavery finally came "tumbling down" as a result of the Civil War, which began in 1861 and ended in 1865.

Three men are depicted in this painting: General Robert E. Lee, President Abraham Lincoln, and General William Tecumseh Sherman. Lee and Sherman were opposing generals who fought in the Civil War when Lincoln was president. The men are surrounded by artifacts now found at the Smithsonian Institute in Washington, DC: a teacup from which President Lincoln drank and a towel used by the Confederate army to signal its surrender. What other items do you see? Why might the artist have included them?

Oh, Peter, Go Ring Them Bells

From Wheeling, West Virginia, to New Orleans, Louisiana, slave auctions began with the tolling of market bells. These were the same markets where meats, grain, vegetables, and livestock were sold. Auctioneers would ring the bell again after each slave was bid upon and the sale was finalized.

Yet bells also ring on happy occasions. In a farming village in northern New York, bells rang to celebrate the end of the Civil War. This painting—and the song's lyrics—reference Saint Peter, an angel who is said to greet people at the gates of heaven. What other signs of joy do you see in the painting?

A NOTE ABOUT THIS BOOK

Most picture books begin with a manuscript written by an author, but not this one. *Like a Bird* started with artist Michele Wood's vision of paintings inspired by slave songs. She asked Cynthia Grady to collaborate. Wood listened and researched. Then she painted. Grady listened and researched and studied the paintings. Then she wrote.

Spirituals are beautiful and often uplifting, but historians agree that they do not mean enslaved Africans felt happy. The songs were also not a way of coping with the horrors of slavery. Spirituals grew out of cultural traditions and religious beliefs—first African and later, American. Former slave and abolitionist Frederick Douglass was concerned about how slavery and slave songs would be understood by later generations. He wrote, "Slaves sing most when they are most unhappy. The songs of the slave represent the sorrows of his heart."

LYRICS

Because spirituals were created spontaneously and sung by thousands of individuals over several centuries, their lyrics have changed over time. Some verses have been forgotten, and some others have been added as musicians began to record them. The lyrics below are some of the earliest recorded, and they remain in the public domain.

Sometimes I Feel Like a Motherless Child

Sometimes I feel like a motherless child,
Sometimes I feel like a motherless child,
Sometimes I feel like a motherless child,
A long way from home.

Sometimes I feel like I'm almost gone,
Sometimes I feel like I'm almost gone,
Sometimes I feel like I'm almost gone,
A long way from home.

Sometimes I feel like a motherless child,
Sometimes I feel like a motherless child,
Sometimes I feel like a motherless child,
A long way from home.

Ezekiel Saw the Wheel

Ezekiel saw the wheel
Way up in the middle of the air
Ezekiel saw the wheel
Way in the middle of the air
The big wheel moved by faith
The little wheel moved by the grace of God
A wheel in a wheel
Way in the middle of the air
Just let me tell you what a hypocrite'll do
Way in the middle of the air
He'll talk about me and he'll talk about you
Way in the middle of the air
Watch out my sister how you walk on the cross
Way in the middle of the air
Your foot might slip and your soul get lost
Way in the middle of the air
You say the Lord has set you free
Way in the middle of the air
Why don't you let your neighbor be
Way in the middle of the air?

Jacob's Ladder

We are climbing Jacob's ladder,
We are climbing Jacob's ladder,
We are climbing Jacob's ladder,
Soldier of the cross.

Ev'ry round goes higher, higher,
Ev'ry round goes higher, higher,
Ev'ry round goes higher, higher,
Soldier of the cross.

Brother, do you love my Jesus,
Brother, do you love my Jesus,
Brother, do you love my Jesus,
Soldier of the cross.

If you love him, why not serve him,
If you love him, why not serve him,
If you love him, why not serve him,
Soldier of the cross.

Michael, Row the Boat Ashore

Michael, row the boat ashore,
Hallelujah!
Then you'll hear the trumpet blow,
Hallelujah!
Then you'll hear the trumpet sound,
Hallelujah!
Trumpet sound the world around,
Hallelujah!
Trumpet sound the jubilee,
Hallelujah!
Trumpet sound for you and me,
Hallelujah!

Nobody Knows the Trouble I've Seen

Nobody knows the trouble I've seen,
Nobody knows but Jesus,
Nobody knows the trouble I've seen,
Glory Hallelujah!

Sometimes I'm up, sometimes I'm down,
Oh, yes, Lord,
Sometimes I'm almost to the ground,
Oh, yes, Lord

Nobody knows the trouble I've seen,
Nobody knows but Jesus,
Nobody knows the trouble I've seen,
Glory Hallelujah!

If you get there before I do,
Oh, yes, Lord,
Tell all my friends I'm coming too,
Oh, yes, Lord

Nobody knows the trouble I've seen,
Nobody knows but Jesus,
Nobody knows the trouble I've seen,
Glory Hallelujah!

Go Down, Moses

When Israel was in Egypt's land,
Let my people go,
Oppressed so hard they could not stand,
Let my people go.

Go down, Moses,
Way down in Egypt's land
Tell old Pharaoh,
To let my people go!

"Thus said the Lord," bold Moses said,
Let my people go,
"If not, I'll smite your firstborn dead,"
Let my people go.

Go down, Moses,
Way down in Egypt's land
Tell old Pharaoh,
To let my people go!

Get On Board—
the Gospel Train

The Gospel train's a-coming,
I hear it just at hand,
I hear the car wheel rumbling,
And rolling through the land.

Get on board little children,
Get on board little children,
Get on board little children,
There's room for many more.

I hear the train a-coming,
She's coming round the curve,
She's loosened all her steam and brakes,
And straining every nerve.

The fare is cheap and all can go,
The rich and poor are there,
No second class aboard this train,
No difference in the fare.

Deep River

Deep river, my home is over Jordan,
Deep river, Lord, I want to cross over into campground.
Deep river, my home is over Jordan,
Deep river, Lord, I want to cross over into campground.

Oh, don't you want to go to that gospel feast,
That promised land where all is peace?
Oh, deep river, Lord,
I want to cross over into campground.

Ain't Gonna Study War No More

I'm going to lay down my burdens,
Down by the riverside,
Down by the riverside,
Down by the riverside;
Going to lay down my burdens,
Down by the riverside,
Ain't going to study war no more.

Ain't going to study war no more,
Study war no more,
Study war no more,
Ain't going to study war no more.

I'm going to lay down my sword and shield,
Down by the riverside,
Down by the riverside,
Down by the riverside;
Going to lay down my sword and shield,
Down by the riverside,
Ain't going to study war no more.

Ain't going to study war no more,
Study war no more,
Study war no more,
Ain't going to study war no more.

I'm going to put on my long white robe,
Down by the riverside,
Down by the riverside,
Down by the riverside,
Going to put on my long white robe,
Down by the riverside;
Ain't going to study war no more.

Ain't going to study war no more,
Study war no more,
Study war no more,
Ain't going to study war no more.

Swing Low, Sweet Chariot

Swing low, sweet chariot,
Coming for to carry me home,
Swing low, sweet chariot,
Coming for to carry me home.

I looked over Jordan, and what did I see,
Coming for to carry me home?
A band of angels coming after me,
Coming for to carry me home.

If you get there before I do,
Coming for to carry me home,
Tell all my friends I'm coming too,
Coming for to carry me home.

Steal Away

Steal away, steal away, steal away to Jesus!
Steal away, steal away home
I ain't got long to stay here!

My Lord, He calls me,
He calls me by the thunder,
The trumpet sounds within-a my soul,
I ain't got long to stay here.

Green trees are bending,
Poor sinners stand a-trembling;
The trumpet sounds within-a my soul,
I ain't got long to stay here.

Joshua Fit the Battle of Jericho

Joshua fit the battle of Jericho, Jericho,
   Jericho:
Joshua fit the battle of Jericho,
And the walls came tumbling down.

You may talk about your king of Gideon,
You may talk about your man of Saul.
There's none like good old Joshua,
At the battle of Jericho.

Up to the walls of Jericho,
He marched with spear in hand.
"Go blow those ram horns," Joshua cried,
"'Cause the battle is in my hands."

Then the lamb, ram, sheep horns begin
   to blow,
Trumpets begin to sound.
Joshua commanded the children to
   shout,
And the walls came tumbling down, that
   morning

Joshua fit the battle of Jericho, Jericho,
   Jericho:
Joshua fit the battle of Jericho,
And the walls came tumbling down.

Oh, Peter, Go Ring Them Bells

Oh, Peter, go ring them bells,
Peter, go ring them bells,
Peter, go ring them bells,
I heard from heaven today.
I wonder where my mother is gone,
I wonder where my mother is gone,
I wonder where my mother is gone,
I heard from heaven today.

I heard from heaven today,
I heard from heaven today,
I thank God and I thank you too,
I heard from heaven today.
Oh, Peter, go ring them bells,
Peter, go ring them bells,
Peter, go ring them bells,
I heard from heaven today.

GLOSSARY

abolitionist: a person who worked to bring about the end of slavery

archangel: an angel of high rank

auctioneer: a person who runs an auction

Babylonia: a country that once existed in the Middle East, located in part of present-day Iraq

baptism: a ritual to purify a person, such as the ritual making a person a part of the Christian church. Baptism involves placing water on a person's head or immersing a person's body in water.

bondage: slavery

Canaan: a country that once existed where present-day Lebanon, Syria, Jordan, and Israel are located

Christian: a person who follows the teachings of Jesus

despair: great sadness and lack of hope

enslaved: a person who is owned by another and is made to work without pay

fare: money paid to ride a train

fit: fought

folk song: a song created by people living in a certain region or country

Gideon: a figure in the Bible who fought to free the Israelites from the Midianites

hallelujah: an exclamation of joy and thanks to God

harmony: the combination of musical notes played or sung at the same time

Hebrew: a member of an ancient group of people who lived mostly in the kingdom of Israel and practiced Judaism

Hebrew scriptures: writings that make up the Bible's Old Testament. They include many stories about the Hebrew people in ancient times.

hypocrite: a person who says one thing but does another

improvise: to make up on the spot

interpret: to depict in a way that shows one's own thoughts, feelings, and beliefs

Israelite: a person who was born in or lived in the ancient kingdom of Israel

Jericho: a city in ancient Palestine

Jesus of Nazareth: the figure in the Bible whose life and teachings inspired the creation of Christianity. Christians believe Jesus is the son of God.

Joshua: a figure in the Bible who led the Israelite army in destroying the city of Jericho

lyrics: the words of a song

Moses: a figure in the Bible who leads the Israelites out of slavery in Egypt

New Testament: the second part of the Christian Bible, which includes stories about Jesus

North Star: a bright star in the northern sky that travelers can use to determine which way is north

pharaoh: a ruler in ancient Egypt

plantation: a large farm in the southern United States that usually used slave labor

River Jordan: a river that runs along the eastern border of Israel

Saint Peter: one of the disciples of Jesus and the angel who is said to greet people arriving at the gates of heaven

Saul: the first king of the kingdom of Israel

scholar: a person who has studied a subject for a long time

smite: to kill

spiritual: a religious folk song originally created by enslaved African Americans in the southern United States

spoke: a bar that connects the center of a wheel to the rim

syncopation: a musical rhythm in which the stress shifts from the strong beat to the weaker beat

toll: to ring

Underground Railroad: a secret network of people who helped slaves escape to freedom

worship: to show love and respect for a god, especially by singing or praying

SELECTED BIBLIOGRAPHY

Carpenter, Delores, and Nolan E. Williams, Jr., eds. *African American Heritage Hymnal*. Chicago: GIA, 2001.

Allen, William Francis, Charles Pickard Ware, and Lucy McKim Garrison, eds. *Slave Songs of the United States* (1867). Electronic ed. *Documenting the American South*. Accessed April 4, 2013. http://docsouth.unc.edu/church/allen/allen/html.

Bradford, Sarah H. *Harriet: The Moses of Her People* (1886). Electronic ed. *Documenting the American South*. Accessed July 29, 2013. http://docsouth/unc.edu/neh/harriet.html.

Fisher, Miles Mark. *Negro Slave Songs in the United States*. New York: Carol Publishing, 1990.

Giovanni, Nikki. *On My Journey Now: Looking at African-American History through the Spirituals*. Cambridge, MA: Candlewick, 2007.

Johnson, James Weldon, and J. Rosemond Johnson. *The Books of American Negro Spirituals*. New York: Viking, 1942.

Jones, Arthur C. *Wade in the Water: The Wisdom of the Spirituals*. Maryknoll, NY: Orbis, 1993.

Jones, Ferdinand, and Arthur C. Jones, eds. *The Triumph of the Soul: Cultural and Psychological Aspects of African American Music*. Westport, CT: Praeger, 2001.

Peretti, Burton W. *Lift Every Voice: The History of African American Music*. Lanham, MD: Rowman & Littlefield, 2009.

Reagon, Bernice Johnson. *If You Don't Go, Don't Hinder Me*. Lincoln: University of Nebraska Press, 2001.

FURTHER READING

Books

Bryan, Ashley. *Let It Shine: Three Favorite Spirituals.* New York: Atheneum Books for Young Readers, 2007.
The lyrics and music to three spirituals are illustrated with vibrant paper collages.

Cooper, Michael L. *Slave Spirituals and the Jubilee Singers.* New York: Clarion, 2001.
This book tells the story of the singers at Fisk University in Tennessee, who traveled and sang to raise money for their university, bringing the slave songs to audiences around the world.

Evans, Shane W. *Underground: Finding the Light to Freedom.* New York: Roaring Brook, 2011.
Told from the point of view of a group of slaves, this picture book follows the group's journey to freedom.

Grady, Cynthia. *I Lay My Stitches Down: Poems of American Slavery.* Grand Rapids, MI: Eerdmans Books for Young Readers, 2012.
Poems and paintings explore the varied experiences of enslaved African Americans.

Rockwell, Anne. *A Spy Called James: The True Story of James Lafayette, Revolutionary War Double Agent.* Minneapolis: Carolrhoda Books, 2016.
Learn more about James Lafayette's work as a spy and find out how he eventually became free.

Weatherford, Carole Boston. *Moses: When Harriet Tubman Led Her People to Freedom.* New York: Hyperion Books for Children, 2006.
Poetic text and stunning artwork present Harriet Tubman, focusing on her religious inspiration as well as her escape to freedom and her role in the Underground Railroad.

Websites

African American Spirituals
http://www.loc.gov/item/ihas.200197495
This Library of Congress page gives an in-depth look at spirituals and provides links to recordings of a number of songs including "Swing Low, Sweet Chariot," "Sometimes I Feel Like a Motherless Child," and "Go Down, Moses."

Fisk Jubilee Singers
http://www.fiskjubileesingers.org/our_history.html
Read about the origins of the Jubilee Singers and find links to more information about this historic group—including a schedule of upcoming performances.

Jubilee Songs
http://www.pbs.org/wgbh/amex/singers/sfeature/songs.html
This page includes links to five spirituals performed by the Jubilee Singers, including "Steal Away" and "Swing Low, Sweet Chariot."

National Park Service: Network to Freedom
http://www.nps.gov/subjects/ugrr/discover_history/index.htm
Read about the history of the Underground Railroad and follow links to a timeline, a map, photographs, and more.

The Rankin House
http://www.ripleyohio.net/htm/rankin.htm
Find out more about the Rankin House in Ripley, Ohio, as well as abolitionist John Rankin.

Sweet Chariot: The Story of the Spirituals
http://spiritualsproject.org/sweetchariot/
This site, which was created by the University of Denver, presents information about the history of spirituals and much more, including recordings and explanations of songs.